On Behalf of Children

Linda Isham

AF251161

JUDSON PRESS
Valley Forge

On Behalf of Children

I'm grateful to many co-workers for critical
reading, helpful feedback,
typing, and above all encouragement!

ON BEHALF OF CHILDREN

Copyright © 1975
Judson Press, Valley Forge, PA 19481

Bible quotations in this book are taken from *Good News for Modern Man, The New Testament in Today's English Version.* Copyright by the American Bible Society, 1966.

Library of Congress Cataloging in Publication Data

Isham, Linda.
  On behalf of children.

  Bibliography: p.
  1. Church work with children. I. Title.
BV639.C4I8   268'.432   74-17842
ISBN 0-8170-0666-4

Printed in the U.S.A.

Introduction

This book has evolved from—

reflecting on experiences with children and with adults who minister with children,

reading that has confirmed hunches I had,

discussion with my co-workers,

review comments by some 145 persons who read an eleven-page "synopsis" of this book.

A cartoon by Morrie Turner triggered the idea for the title *On Behalf of Children.* (© King Features Syndicate, 1972)

Basic to the title *On Behalf of Children* is my assumption that we act most authentically on behalf of children when we—

have shared experiences with them,
see them as persons,
seek to act cooperatively with them,
and maintain a responsible, caring adult role.

The intent of this book is to explore what it means to act authentically on behalf of children and to offer a vehicle for reflection, dialogue, and action to persons concerned for the church's ministry with children. Space is provided throughout the book to facilitate your dialogue reflection.

This book makes a statement of who we (children and adults) are and what we can do together as people of God. This book makes a statement for NOW—recognizing that as time goes on we'll learn more about children and our ministry and that future statements will be made. This book suggests ways persons can plan for and minister with children in their midst.

I invite you to—

read this book,
make marginal notes,
agree and disagree,
recall children you know,
recall your own experiences,
discuss it with others,
observe and interact with children,
evaluate your own ministry with children,

and

act on behalf of children.

Contents

1. Today's Children

Some people brought children to Jesus for him to touch, but the disciples scolded those people. When Jesus noticed it, he was angry and said to his disciples, "Let the children come to me, and do not stop them, because the Kingdom of God belongs to such as these. Remember this! Whoever does not receive the Kingdom of God like a child will never enter it." Then he took the children in his arms, placed his hands on each of them, and blessed them. (Mark 10:13-16)

Let's begin by considering children—what it's like for them today, what it may be like tomorrow, what they need, and what they offer to adults.

When I stop to consider children, four specific children come to my mind. They happen to be a nephew and three nieces ranging in age from five to ten years. They have much in common, and yet at the same time each is a unique person. Each grows at his/her own rate and pace. Each responds differently to each new situation that is faced.

STOP READING FOR A MOMENT. RECALL A CHILD OR CHILDREN YOU KNOW. Build a picture in your mind. . . .
  Name them
  Describe what they look like, what they say and/or do

Having focused on a specific child or children that you know, let's move on to consider children in a broader sense. Don't lose sight of the children you know. Refer to them as you read. Let them be concrete examples and points of reference for you.

ENVIRONMENT

In the past parents, family, school, church, and peers played the significant roles in influencing children. Today's children, though still influenced by their immediate environments, are greatly influenced by an environment beyond family, school, and church. Part of that larger environment is brought about by mass media, television in particular.

When I was young my environment was pretty much bound by my family, the kids on the block, one public school, Sunday church school, a downtown within walking distance, an occasional trip by car to visit relatives in a neighboring state, the radio, and an occasional movie. Life seemed to be more simple and rural. There was an established routine for daily living. Choices were few.

Today my nieces' and nephew's environment is bound by an extended family, kids in the neighborhood, two public schools and one private school, Sunday church school, shopping centers in three different directions, dependency on the automobile to get to school and to extracurricular activities, proximity to two huge metropolitan areas, TV, and relatives in Pennsylvania, California, and Wisconsin.

There is great diversity in the environments of children today. Some children live in isolated rural worlds exposed to family and a small group of peers much like themselves, far from the urban areas. Others live in isolated urban areas where they know only a few city blocks and others who live much as they do. Some have known only poverty, some comfort, some even wealth. Occasionally the environments cross and mix. Many children have traveled extensively and have had tastes of other environments.

Television has exposed most children to a broader view of the world and may have helped to speed up their rate of intellectual development. Halfway around the world can seem to be next door, and simulated experiences can seem to be real and true. TV can keep children away from actual experiences and relationships with persons. TV can offer distorted or conflicting values for children.

Today's children are influenced to a greater degree than before by many other persons in addition to their parents. Today's children live in an environment that is very complex, constantly changing, sometimes confusing, and often challenging.

What does the future hold? The future, while it offers hope, is not without its major problems for children. Dr. Chester Pierce of Harvard's School of Medicine, in a presentation to the Association for Childhood Education International in April, 1972, described some of what he sees as the hope in the future for children: a longer life span, advanced thinking skills, a single, universal language, and more leisure time. He also noted some problems that will probably be faced: limited resources, density of population, pollution of the environment, regulation of personality and society, and racism. To live with both the hope and problems, Dr. Pierce suggests that children will need to (1) develop skills of decision-making, communication, collaboration, and an attitude that suggests there is more than one way to get to where they're going; and (2) have a sense that they are related to, are a part of, and must care for the entire world.

HOW WOULD YOU DESCRIBE THE ENVIRONMENT OF THE CHILDREN YOU KNOW AND WITH WHOM YOU MINISTER?

WHAT DOES THEIR FUTURE ENVIRONMENT LOOK LIKE?

NEEDS

Children, no matter what environment they live in, share some common needs. Those needs can be classified within three broad areas: physical, social-emotional, and intellectual. Quite obviously the needs and the degree to which they are met vary from child to child.

Physical Needs

The physical needs of children are the most obvious. Their needs for shelter, food, and clothing must be cared for. We can't assume that all children have these needs met. Some children are inadequately sheltered and clothed. Many lack appropriate nutrition, and some suffer from malnutrition.

Closely related to the need to be cared for physically is the right of children to be free from physical harm and abuse. In recent years the number, or at least the awareness, of cases of battered and abused children seems to have increased. We can no longer assume that all children are free from physical abuse, often inflicted by a parent.

Social-Emotional Needs

We can describe the social-emotional need as the need to be loved and to love. That's not enough! We ought to be more specific in describing this need.

Children seek acceptance as persons of worth. They want to be seen as persons with contributions to make. They need to be valued and respected.

Children need to be touched and to be held. They need to be mothered and fathered. Particularly as infants, they need to feel secure. Experiments with hospitalized infants have proved that without "mothering" and the development of *trust* infants do not develop normally, and sometimes they die.

Children need to be free to develop a sense of self. They need to begin between the second and fourth years to say "I want this and I want that." A familiar illustration of this need is found in the two-year-old who responds to many requests with a strong, "No!"; or with a four-year-old I know who says, "I can do it myself!" This response is a move for *independence*. It takes a certain amount of courage because the child must risk displeasing his/her parents.

Sometime around the age of four to six years a child has a need to *identify* with persons of the same sex; for most children that means with a parent of the same sex. I see this in a young friend of mine. At the beginning of her year in second grade I talked with her on the phone. I asked her how school was. She replied, "It's beau-u-tiful! I lo-v-e my teacher!" Her teacher was a woman and provided a model in addition to the one offered by her mother.

In the latter years of childhood, there is a need to surrender one's self-centered good for the good of the group. This is the need to belong to a community, to *conform,* to obey the law. I see it in the eight- or nine-year-old's interest in organized groups and games.

Intellectual Needs

Intellectually, children need to have many and varied experiences.

They need to be stimulated. They need to sense many things by touching, tasting, smelling, hearing, and seeing.

Children also need opportunities to explore and discover meanings. They need to find out for themselves, to learn by trial and error, to fail, and to succeed.

D. Campbell Wyckoff suggests that the primary learning tasks of childhood are exploring and discovering meanings. He goes on to say that "in Christian education the chief task of childhood is perceiving the gospel. This means exploring the gospel (seeing, hearing, getting acquainted), experimenting with the gospel (activities and projects in which one's ideas and insights are tried out), and organizing and refining one's thoughts and feelings on the gospel (thought, prayer, talk)." [1]

Experiencing and exploring many things leads to recognizing and then labeling those experiences—all contributing to language development. For example, a young child meets and plays with a dog. After several such encounters the child recognizes a dog when he/she sees one and eventually calls that animal by the word "dog." And some day the child will learn to write and spell that same word, will learn that dogs are part of a complex animal kingdom and have varying roles in human civilization.

While faith development is not totally intellectual, the process is similar to what's been described in the preceding paragraphs. Experiencing and exploring leads to recognizing and labeling. The child learns the language of faith by experiencing it.

LIST NEEDS YOU OBSERVE IN CHILDREN YOU KNOW.
Physical:

Social-emotional:

Intellectual:

[1] D. Campbell Wyckoff, *Learning Tasks in the Curriculum* (Valley Forge: Board of Educational Ministries, American Baptist Churches, U.S.A., 1965), p. 26.

GIFTS

It has been my experience to find myself and others caught in the box of teaching and tending to the needs of children and all too frequently being insensitive to gifts children bring to us. By gifts I mean the intangible, attitudinal offerings, resources, and strengths. Perhaps we fail to see and receive the gifts of children because we are often unable to recognize and admit our own gifts and those of other adults.

It occurred to me as I was writing about the needs of children that many of those needs could be looked at from the other side as gifts.

Trust,
 independence,
  identification,
  conformity

in children are gifts to us if we are able to receive them in the moment that they are given. They are like a two-sided coin. Heads, I love you. Tails, I need to be loved.

The infant, though requiring a lot of our time in order to have his/her physical needs met, gives himself/herself to us for care. The young, independent child is making the break from total dependence, thus giving us a break. Finding ourselves the model for an early elementary-age child is both affirming and demanding. Older children show us that they are able to look beyond themselves and we rejoice. Yet we sometimes are concerned with the strong peer influence in their lives.

In reflecting on gifts children bring, I listed the four which follow. They don't happen to be gifts necessarily unique to childhood. But they are, I think, more evident in the child than in the adult. They are meant to be illustrative and not necessarily conclusive.

BEFORE YOU READ FURTHER TAKE A PIECE OF PAPER AND LIST GIFTS YOU HAVE RECEIVED IN THE LAST MONTH FROM CHILDREN.

OKAY, LET'S COMPARE OUR LISTS.

---

1. *New ways of seeing the commonplace.* Let me illustrate from my own experience. Two summers ago my nephew, who was then eight, came to visit. While he was visiting, we went to a nearby shopping center. Now I go there frequently but always with the clear intention to shop and get out of there as quickly as I can. On that day I saw fountains, sculpture, cannons, and stained glass that I had never seen before. It was as if my nephew had opened to me an entirely new world in that very familiar shopping center.

2. *Affection freely given.* Again let me illustrate. Think of the times when you've gone to visit friends or family and the children have run out the door and greeted you with spontaneous hugs; or in the course of the visit one has whispered, "I love you."

3. *Creative spontaneous ideas.* I recall the time one summer when my niece, then six, came for a visit. As we were driving from her home to mine, I suggested we play some games. We did play some that I suggested, and then she suggested two of her own—made up on the spot and appropriate for two people traveling in a car.

4. *Uninhibited expression.* A friend told me of a conversation he had overheard while he was attending a concert of the Philadelphia Orchestra at the Academy of Music in Philadelphia. As the conductor, Eugene Ormandy, was walking to the podium, a man turned to the child with him and said, "That's Eugene Ormandy, one of the best music leaders in the world." And in reply the child said, "Let's go, Organdy!"

In her book *Eighth Day of Creation,* Elizabeth O'Connor suggests that one of the reasons we have difficulty identifying our gifts is that we have had no one to listen to us or even look at us. She goes on to say that as adults our task with children is to listen to them—that includes receiving the gifts they offer. "Instead of telling our children what they should do and become, we must be humble before their wisdom, believing that in them and not in us is the secret that they need to discover."[2]

REFLECT ON THE GIFTS CHILDREN BRING YOU. HOW CAN YOU ENCOURAGE THE GIVING AND RECEIVING OF SUCH GIFTS?

REFLECT ON CHILDREN, THEIR ENVIRONMENT, NEEDS, AND GIFTS.
Spend some time with children . . .
> **observing,**
> **listening,**
> **sharing.**

COMPLETE A SIMILE
Being a child in today's world is like. . . .

PRETEND FOR A MOMENT THAT YOU'RE A CHILD (PICK AN AGE).
What's your world like? What are your needs? Your gifts?

---

[2]Elizabeth O'Connor, *Eighth Day of Creation: Gifts and Creativity* (Waco, Texas: Word, Inc., 1971), pp. 17-19.

2. Growing, Developing Persons

And the child grew and became strong; he was full of wisdom, and God's blessings were with him. (Luke 2:40)

Children are persons. They have qualities in common with all persons as well as some that make them children. They are growing, developing persons in a particular age-group—birth to twelve years. They are participants in the world in which they live. They grow as they interact with their environment. They are *not* pre-adults. They are involved in childhood, a very important stage of growth in and of itself.

Childhood is a beginning for
creeping, crawling, walking,
climbing, and jumping,
throwing a ball and catching it,
writing with a pencil.
Childhood is a beginning for
touching, tasting, smelling, hearing, and seeing,
knowing what you've sensed,
telling someone about the things you know,
and
asking about what you don't know.
Childhood is a time to begin
trusting,
saying yes or no,
being fond of your teacher,
giving up something you want for someone else.

Childhood has its own significant aspects, yet it is related to other stages of development and builds toward them.

STOP. RECALL YOUR OWN CHILDHOOD—Focus in on a particular age.
What did you enjoy most?

What worried you?

NOW OBSERVE CHILDREN ABOUT YOU.

There are many theories of child development. Most theorists will agree that certain stages of development are alike for all children though each child's pattern and rate of growth is individual. Each child's developing self interacts with his/her environment, and his/her life is shaped. Each child inherits a unique set of physical/social-emotional/intellectual endowments. No single child is exactly like another.

The accompanying chart (Chart A) will serve to describe some developmental stages in childhood. It is divided into three aspects of development: physical, social-emotional, and intellectual. Together they describe an integrated or whole approach to development. They are arbitrarily separated here to help us look at the component parts. Each aspect is interrelated with each other aspect. Physical development affects intellectual development. Being able to read, for example, is dependent on both physical and intellectual development and can be dependent on one's social-emotional development as well.

AS YOU STUDY THE CHART THINK OF DIFFERENT CHILDREN YOU KNOW.
What have been their rates and patterns of growth?

You'll note that in Chart A there is not a column labeled religious development. Development in the Christian faith does not happen

	NURSERY Birth-1	NURSERY 2-3 years	KINDERGARTEN 4-5 years	PRIMARY Grades 1-2	MIDDLER Grades 3-4	JUNIOR Grades 5-6
PHYSICAL DEVELOPMENT[1]	Crawls	Talks Walks Exercises bladder control	Develops large muscles	Develops small muscles and eye-hand coordination		
SOCIAL-EMOTIONAL DEVELOPMENT[2]	Trusts	Demonstrates independence		Identifies with parent of same sex	Conforms to group ideas, goals, etc.	
INTELLECTUAL DEVELOPMENT[3]		Is self-centered Senses and recognizes experiences Can't relate one fact to another Can't check whether or not mistaken		Is less self-centered Thinks concretely Sometimes makes generalizations Sometimes checks conclusions		Is other-centered Thinks abstractly Makes generalizations Checks conclusions

For further study see:

1. Gladys Gardner Jenkins, Helen S. Shacter, William W. Bauer, *These Are Your Children: A Text and Guide on Child Development,* 3rd ed. Glenview, Ill.: Scott, Foresman and Company, 1966.
2. Charles William Stewart, *Adolescent Religion: A Developmental Study of the Religion of Youth* (Chapter 12, "Faith and Coping Styles"). Nashville, Tenn.: Abingdon Press, 1967.
3. Ronald Goldman, *Readiness for Religion: A Basis for Developmental Religious Education.* New York: The Seabury Press, 1970.

apart from all other development. A child's faith develops as he/she grows physically, socially-emotionally, and intellectually. The following chart (Chart B) seeks to show that faith development is dependent on all other areas of development. This chart will speak to four areas of faith response: relationship to God through Jesus, relationship to the church, relationship to the Bible, and relationship to others.

Charles William Stewart has suggested that the following—
    trust,
        independence,
            identification,
                conformity—
are roots of faith.[1] But to stop at the point of conformity leaves us with an unfinished picture of what's needed in the development of faith. A faith which stops at the point of conformity is incomplete. A person must go on to discover a sense of identity, to discover an ultimate loyalty, to commit oneself—to experience faith in a way that is personally authentic, within and beyond conformity.

Trust, independence, identification, conformity, and self-identity may be seen as roots of faith for all ages. It is generally assumed that discovering a sense of personal identity is the dominant task for adolescents and that developing trust, independence, identification, and conformity are primary tasks of children. These roots continue to be important throughout our lives.

RECALL YOUR OWN DEVELOPMENT IN THE CHRISTIAN FAITH—your memories of prayer, reading the Bible, sharing, church school teachers, becoming a follower of Jesus Christ.

AT WHAT POINTS DOES CHART B DESCRIBE MOST ACCURATELY/LEAST ACCURATELY YOUR OWN GROWTH IN FAITH?

Does it reflect accurately the faith development of children you know?

---

[1] Charles William Stewart, *Adolescent Religion: A Developmental Study of the Religion of Youth* (Nashville, Tenn.: Abingdon Press, 1967), pp. 248-269.

RELATIONSHIP TO GOD THROUGH JESUS

NURSERY Birth- 3 years	Abstract thinking is not possible for young children, so God and Jesus often seem the same to them. Through pictures and stories about Jesus, they begin to know him as a loving person, best communicated to them by loving adults. God as the creator of the natural wonders which they discover is perhaps their first concept of God.
KINDERGARTEN 4-5 years	These children identify most with the baby Jesus, God's gift to us. They respond to the drama and excitement of his birth because birthdays are important to them, theirs and those of brothers and sisters. They know Jesus grew and became a kind man. They sense a loving God through the adults who share this feeling with them as they live together in the community of the committed.
PRIMARY Grades 1-2	These children identify with the boy Jesus: the growing Boy at home, at school, in the carpenter shop. He becomes a model for them. They sense that Jesus had a relationship with God in his growing years; hence they can have one also. They feel that they can tell God anything. They can recognize that God loves them just as they are. They often want to thank God, the Creator, for his wonderful world.
MIDDLER Grades 3-4	Since these children are especially interested in what is **"real,"** they see Jesus as a teacher directly related to people in everyday acts. They begin to recognize that Jesus knew more about God than anyone else and that he was able to live the way God wants people to live. Like the six- and seven-year-olds, they feel that they can tell God anything. They, too, are especially aware of God as creator.
JUNIOR Grades 5-6	These are the years when children seek heroes whom they want to follow. For many juniors, Jesus Christ becomes the man of action who knew what God is like, and they want to follow him. Personal relationships are important to juniors, and they want to belong with his "followers." These children want to respond in action. It is a time for serving God by helping people.

RELATIONSHIP TO THE CHURCH

Young children need the security of familiar surroundings and faces. At church that means a room for them and continuity in the persons who care for and teach them. They experience the church within their room and the persons who minister there. Those persons communicate feelings and attitudes about the church by what they say and do. A child's own attitude about the church will be shaped in part by these early contacts.

Familiar surroundings and faces are welcomed by kindergartners even as they try out their own independence. Continuity in adults who minister with them is important. The children will experience the church in their own group but can understand that the church includes others who study and worship in the same building. They can see the minister as a leader of the congregation.

For children who are beginning to identify with persons of the same sex, both male and female models become important. Their understanding of the church and relationship to it are being shaped in part by their observation of adults.

For primary children the church becomes more than a place. A picture of the church as a group of people who worship, study, work, and serve others is beginning to take shape. They can experience many more things within the life of the church. They can participate in congregational worship in addition to their own class activities. They can become aware that the church carries on the ministry of Jesus. Their relationship to the church continues in part to be shaped by the attitudes and behavior of the adults who minister with them. Both male and female models are needed for children of this age.

Third- and fourth-graders are developing a sense of the church as a fellowship of people who gather to work, worship, and study and scatter to serve others. They can understand that the church continues the work of Jesus and that people within the church have a special understanding of and relationship to Jesus. They can participate in the worship and various projects of giving. Being a part of a group of peers is important to most children this age. Working together on service projects for others can provide meaningful learning. Through such efforts they can begin to sense that they are related to a fellowship wider than their own local church.

It is important for juniors to participate in the fellowship, work, study, worship, and service of the church. Although they can understand the larger fellowship of the church and its ministry, involvement with their own peers is the way they best express their part in the life of the church. They can assume responsibility for the care of property and for giving part of their own earnings for the work of the church. A beginning sense of loyalty to a group beyond themselves and their peers is developing. Some will choose to commit themselves to Jesus Christ and join the church.

RELATIONSHIP TO THE BIBLE

NURSERY **Birth- 3 years**	Children two and three years of age can listen to selected Bible stories—stories about real people and about experiences appropriate to children this age. Seeing adults use the Bible, these children can sense that the Bible is an important book to adults in the church.
KINDERGARTEN **4-5 years**	Children of ages four and five continue to enjoy selected Bible stories. They can recognize that stories about God and Jesus are found in the Bible. They, too, are aware that the Bible is a special book to the church. They can remember and repeat short Bible verses appropriate to the focus of a given session.
PRIMARY **Grades 1-2**	Primary children enjoy Bible stories. They can relate some Bible stories to their own experiences. As they learn to read, they can find familiar words in the Bible. Some advanced readers can read short portions of the Bible. These children can remember and repeat larger portions of Scripture.
MIDDLER **Grades 3-4**	Because reading skills are developing, most children of this age can read from the Bible. Thus it's an appropriate time for the congregation to give a copy of the Bible to each child. It's a time, too, to help children learn to use the Bible. They can relate stories in the Bible to many of their own experiences. They can remember such Scriptures as the Lord's Prayer and feel a part of the church as it shares such passages in corporate worship.
JUNIOR **Grades 5-6**	Juniors can read from the Bible and understand much of the continuity and unity of its message. They can relate stories and passages to their own experiences and those of others. They can use the Bible to help interpret life issues and to guide their daily living. Sometimes they question stories as written and often still need help in interpreting symbolic and abstract thoughts.

RELATIONSHIP TO OTHERS

Young children are self-centered. It is difficult for them to share or play with someone else. They aren't able to see situations from the perspectives of other people. They play by themselves or in parallel fashion with others. They do need opportunities and guidance to learn to share and play together. They need time to try to solve problems for themselves. They do need limits to keep them from hurting other children or property. They are trusting people and need contact with trusting adults within the church. Their experiences with other persons are limited and they need to be introduced gradually to new people.

It's an expanding world for kindergartners. Many are in weekday schools and have many contacts with other children and adults. They are beginning to move from being self-centered, as we can observe in their play with others. Small groupings let them explore playing together within a fairly safe framework. They can share their belongings and are learning to take turns. They can participate in service projects for people that they know.

Adult models of the same sex are important to children of this age. They often imitate the behavior of those adults. Contact with a variety of adults helps them see differences and similarities in people. They can work together on simple short-term service projects. They have a developing keen sense of right and wrong. Abiding by the rules can become important to many children. They feel strongly for those who are hurt or need help.

Working and playing with peers is important and meaningful activity for third and fourth graders. Organized games and clubs are examples of peer group efforts. Making up and/or following the rules is important. Peer group pressure on those who don't is strong. These children are aware of their own strengths and weaknesses and those of others. They are beginning to see that they are related to many people whom they have not even met.

Peer group involvements continue to be important for juniors. They are influenced by peers as well as by adults who offer models to follow. They are developing an increasing sense of respect and concern for others. They are aware that not all people are treated fairly. Their sense of justice is strong, and they want to take action on behalf of justice. They are aware of, interested in, and concerned about persons around the world.

3. Adults Who Minister with Children

There are different kinds of spiritual gifts, but the same Spirit gives them. There are different ways of serving, but it is the same Lord who is served. There are different abilities to perform service, but it is the same God who gives ability to everyone for all services. Each one is given some proof of the Spirit's presence for the good of all.

(1 Corinthians 12:4-7, paraphrased)

Who are we? We are teachers, friends, superintendents, chairpersons of children's ministry, pastors, counselors, parents, crossing guards, and you and me—persons who care for children and act on their behalf. Some of us act in planned teaching-learning events, some of us act spontaneously as the moment presents itself, and some of us act in both ways at different times.

ENVIRONMENT

There is as great diversity among our environments as there is among those of the children with whom we minister. Some of us live in densely populated urban areas, some in sprawling suburbs, some in or near small towns, and some in isolated rural areas.

We come from diverse backgrounds with a variety of experiences and training, with a variety of interests and skills, with varying degrees of commitment, and with a variety of Christian life-styles. Some of us are young, some middle-aged, and some older adults. We interact with our worlds differently. We approach the world differently than children do, because many of us have experienced many different worlds in our lifetimes. Our past experiences color our response to the world today. Because we have experienced more than children have, our responses to our environments are often less spontaneous and more cautious.

For example, I grew up in a small town, went to college in a city, and now live and work in the sprawling suburbs of a large metropolitan area. I've had college, seminary, and in-service training. I've taught nursery, kindergarten, primary, and junior children, youth, and adults. I try to be a listener, and I like to plan and carry out teaching-learning events. I learn about children and childhood from spending time with children. I like to try something out before I say yes to it. I guess that makes me somewhat cautious by nature. But I also think that there is usually more than one way to do something or get somewhere, and I encourage considering options and alternatives.

YOUR TURN. PAUSE. REFLECT FOR A FEW MINUTES ON YOUR WORLD AND YOUR RESPONSE TO IT. How is it like that of other persons? How does your interaction with your environment affect your ministry with children?

We come from many and diverse experiences to our ministry with children. This ministry is enriched by our diversity. We need one another.

NEEDS

As adults we too need shelter, food, and clothing for mere survival. For more abundant living we need to love and be loved. As Christian adults we need a growing faith to sustain us.

As persons who minister with children we need to understand ourselves—what motivates us, what we value, what makes us angry, and what brings us joy. We need to reflect on our faith and to see how it speaks to our lives.

As persons who minister with children we need to understand those with whom we minister—their world, how they grow and develop, and their needs. We need to be ready to be ministered to by children.

As persons who minister with children we are in need of a community of support. We need persons who encourage us, who seek to understand our ministry, who call us into question, and who, through their support, share our ministry. We need to recall that we are united in the body of Christ. We do not minister alone.

I don't know what's true for you, but for me there are times when my need to be supported is greater than at other times. When work at the office stacks up, homework from the course I'm taking accumulates, my apartment needs cleaning, and people make demands, I begin to think that I'm alone, that everything rests on my shoulders. I need the reminder that my work is not dependent on me alone. It's shared by others. There is a source of strength outside myself.

AS ONE WHO MINISTERS WITH CHILDREN, WHAT ARE YOUR NEEDS? Who supports you? How does having your needs met help you minister with children?

GIFTS

In very broad terms, our gifts are two: experience with reflection and a model of commitment to Jesus Christ. These gifts are not solely our possessions, but they are common to us as adults.

Each of us speaks and acts out of varied experiences and out of our reflections on these experiences. We've tried things and learned either that they work or don't work. We know what helps and what hinders something in its operation. We have clues about the consequences if we do certain things. We have learned a lot from our experiences and our reflection on those experiences. We use our gift of experience with reflection to help us plan, choose, make decisions, solve problems, save time and worry, be patient, anticipate possible consequences, and see options open to us.

The thing we must remember is that children too have experiences—though in a more limited way. Our gift cannot be received if it puts down another person's experiences. It must be offered and not imposed. It ceases to be a gift when it's imposed. How often do we offer the gift of "adult insight" in a way that emphasizes the child's lack of understanding?

Each of us offers a model of commitment to Jesus Christ. When it is shared honestly and freely without obligation, it can be received. When children see various models, they have the opportunity to choose which model is appropriate for them to try out.

But individually we offer different things. We offer those gifts that we've identified for ourselves, that have been affirmed by others, and that we put to work. We can't offer a gift if it's still packaged and stored away in our minds. To be received it has to be exposed to the light of day—to be shared with someone—to be given and received.

TAKE SEVERAL MINUTES. FIND A SPOT THAT'S YOURS. Concentrate on that space that's yours. Block out activity around you. Focus on your gifts. What gifts do you have?

TAKE A SHEET OF PAPER. DIVIDE IT INTO TWO COLUMNS: (1) My gifts that are known to others, (2) My gifts that are hidden from others. List gifts in both columns.

Are there gifts in column 2 that could be shared? What would it take for you to begin to share one (or more) of your hidden gifts?

GROWTH AND DEVELOPMENT

Like children, we have qualities in common with all persons. Like children, we are growing, developing persons. We are persons in a rather broad age-group from young to middle to senior adulthood.

Growth for us is not as dramatic and as observable as with children nor as variable as with youth. Our growth is more a matter of refining and maturing. Like children, each of us has his/her own pattern and rate of growth.

Martha Leypoldt in her book *Learning Is Change*[1] suggests some generalizations we can make about adulthood.

1. Adulthood does not begin at a specific age, although we often think of adulthood beginning at age eighteen with the opportunity to vote and graduation from high school. Using age as a criterion has its difficulties when we realize that persons vary so greatly in their maturing. We don't all reach adulthood at the same age.

2. Adulthood involves some degree of continuity and stability. The movement from adolescence to adulthood doesn't happen overnight. At some time, however, we're more continuously independent and stabilized. We no longer waiver between childhood and adulthood.

3. Adulthood involves assuming responsibilities. We make

[1] Martha M. Leypoldt, *Learning Is Change* (Valley Forge: Judson Press, 1971), pp. 9-10.

decisions with regard to employment, life-style, marriage, parenthood, and civic and/or church responsibility. The areas of decision making and assumption of responsibility vary from person to person.

4. Adulthood is a process of becoming. Although some significant events make us feel like adults, for most of us the process of becoming an adult is gradual. Being an adult does not mean we have arrived.

My own experience supports the idea that we reach adulthood in different areas at different times. After finishing school at twenty-five, I took my first full-time job. Somewhere around the age of thirty, I had gained a better understanding of myself as a single adult in a world of mostly couples.

I'm employed by a national church agency. I live alone. I've taught church school. I'm chairperson of the nursery school at our church and a member of the Board of Worship and Life of my church. I'm a registered voter.

I'm also taking courses at a nearby college and have recently taken up gardening. Daily I learn and change. I'm not quite the same person today that I was yesterday.

PAUSE FOR A FEW MOMENTS. RECALL YOUR OWN JOURNEY INTO ADULTHOOD. What significant events mark that journey? What characterizes your growth and development now?

How does seeing yourself as a growing person help you in your ministry with children?

We are more than adults. We are adults involved in ministry with children. We assume responsibility for that ministry and that makes it all the more important that we continue to grow and develop. As teachers or leaders in this ministry, we become intentional about growing and developing: that is, we set goals. We find ways to learn about child development, the Bible, ourselves, teaching methods, etc. We observe others as they teach. We enter into dialogue with others. We read. We evaluate our progress. We learn with children.

4. A Faith to Share

You are like the light for the whole world. . . . No one lights a lamp to put it under a bowl; instead he puts it on the lampstand, where it gives light for everyone in the house. In the same way your light must shine before people, so that they will see the good things you do and give praise to your Father in heaven.

(Matthew 5:14-16)

As adults who minister with children we have a faith to share. It is a faith that has its roots in the message of God's love found in the Bible. It is a faith based on the Lordship of Jesus Christ. It is a faith growing from our own experiences and the experience of the Christian community through the years and in the present. This accumulated faith experience and reflection serves to interpret all of our lives, all of our relationships. It is a faith that is sustained by the community of faith—the church—and refreshed daily by the presence of the Holy Spirit. It is a faith that is open to rethinking, to new insights, to growth.

A growing faith is one that is in process. It is not completed once and for all but evolves as we experience and reflect on life itself. Faith as we understand it helps us interpret all of our lives. No area of our lives or relationships is outside of the faith interpretation.

Our faith has grown in part from the experiences and the testimonies of many people. We have many points of reference and examples to turn to. The record of God's action among persons in the Bible provides us with a norm by which we can measure our living out of the Christian faith. We use it to understand our own life experiences.

As I reflect back on my own pilgrimage in the Christian faith, I am aware of many significant persons: my parents, two adults in the church in which I grew up, a pastor, a high school teacher, a campus minister and his wife, and a seminary professor. For a time in the early years of my childhood and youth, my faith was, in a real sense, that of my parents. The family faith was my faith—secondhand in a way—but it was appropriate for the time. As an adolescent I joined the church. That decision was largely based on my wanting to be in tune with the rest of my peers in the church. As I reflect on it now, it was an appropriate decision at the moment. Since that time I've taken on the Christian faith for myself. It is now a firsthand faith.

RECALL YOUR OWN FAITH PILGRIMAGE FROM CHILDHOOD TO ADULTHOOD (OR FROM THE AGE AT WHICH FAITH BEGAN FOR YOU). What significant experiences stand out for you? When did your faith become firsthand? What persons were important in that pilgrimage? How would you characterize your understanding of your own faith and its expression today?

WHAT WE SHARE

As we live out the Christian faith daily, we make some statements (sometimes spoken, sometimes acted out) about (1) our relationship to God through Jesus Christ, (2) our understanding of persons, (3) the place of the church, and (4) the role of the Bible. Each of us interprets each of these faith components according to our own experiences. We interpret these components whether we speak directly to and about them or act them out intentionally or nonintentionally. Often our actions speak louder than our words. We speak most strongly when the action and the words are in harmony with one another.

Relationship to God Through Jesus Christ

God is creator, redeemer, and sustainer.

God created life and it was good (Genesis 1:31). Persons failed to recognize God as creator. They failed to care for God's creation. They alienated themselves from God (Genesis 3; Luke 15:11-24). God's care continued, and they failed to recognize and receive it.

Then in the person of Jesus Christ, God came to persons in human

28

form (John 1:1-4). God's love and care was uniquely shown in Jesus' life, death, and resurrection. Persons could know God in the example of Jesus Christ. Jesus brought the potential for wholeness to persons.

And today God is present in our lives as the Holy Spirit works in and through us (John 14:16-17).

For me, my relationship to God through Jesus Christ is expressed in giving thanks to God for his gift of life, in sensing and accepting my own wholeness as a person, and in saying yes to what lies ahead without having it all clearly laid out. Sometimes that relationship is broken. But I know that healing comes to the brokenness, reconciliation to the alienation.

Understanding of Persons

What we are talking about here is what we have sometimes called the doctrine of man.

All persons are created in God's image (Genesis 1:27), created with the potential to be whole, responding persons, created to take loving care of God's creation. All have the potential for perceiving God as creator. All have the potential for finding wholeness.

All persons have sinned (Romans 3:21-24). All have failed to see God as creator. All have failed to care for his creation with loving care. But God continues to seek persons and call them to respond. God is persistent in loving and caring. So even though persons sin, the potential for recognizing God as creator and caring for God's creation is still present.

As Christians we recognize in Jesus Christ a person who gave his life for all persons and to whom we can commit ourselves (Acts 2:22-24, 38-39). We seek to respond to God's love by declaring our allegiance to Jesus Christ, by being baptized, and by ministering to others. We try to use the gifts given us to carry out our ministries. We seek to grow and develop our skills to use the gifts God has given us.

I express my understanding of persons by seeking to see and respond to all persons as persons of worth with the right to life. Now sometimes I fail but I'm coming to know that failure is a part of my personhood.

I believe we have the potential for being able to live in mutual caring relationships with others. And I seek to encourage the development of a sense of interdependence among people. I cannot live without you. You cannot live without me. I am not totally dependent on you nor you on me. Together we can live freely and responsibly.

The Place of the Church

The early Christians gathered together for prayer, fellowship, and meals (Acts 2:42). They sought out others who chose to follow Jesus' way. They were a community of believers and doers. The book of Acts is filled with stories of faith and action in that early Christian community.

The church exists to do four things: celebrate (worship individually and corporately), nurture (educate), share (support each other), and serve (witness and minister to others). The church is probably most visible to us in its gathered form; that is, a group of people meeting together and working together through a corporate budget to serve others. The church exists in scattered forms through the varied ministries of its individual members.

For me the idea of the church as a becoming community makes a great deal of sense. It has not arrived. It is human. It is growing. It has potential. Its ministries of celebration, nurturing, sharing, and serving are important for me. It is important to recall my heritage, to give thanks, and to look ahead. It is important to learn what it means to live faithfully. It is important to support others and to be supported. It is important to minister to others in their need.

The Role of the Bible

The Bible provides us with a record of God's action among persons. Written by persons inspired by God it tells us about our heritage, about our faith (John 21:24-25; Luke 1:1-4). Its message is that which we seek to live out. It gives us clues about what our relationship to God through Christ can be, it helps us understand persons, and it serves to describe what the church can be in our lives.

In my own life the Bible serves as a norm, a guide for how I live my life. I read and study it. I try to act out its message and in that way share something of its meaning with others. I see its words as primarily intended for adults. I see its meaning and message intended for all of us, children, youth, adults.

WHAT STATEMENTS DO YOU MAKE ABOUT (remember a statement is sometimes spoken, sometimes acted out):

1. Your relationship to God through Jesus Christ?

2. Your understanding of persons?

3. The place of the church for you?

4. The role of the Bible in your life?

TURN BACK TO CHART B AND CONSIDER THE RESPONSES CHILDREN CAN MAKE TO THE FOUR COMPONENTS.

HOW WE SHARE OUR FAITH

We've looked at the faith we share. Now let's consider how we share it.

In Spontaneous Unplanned Ways

Spontaneous ways of sharing our faith are person-to-person. They are not planned for. They happen. They may occur within a planned teaching-learning event; they may occur on a street corner, in a backyard, in the church corridor, in the schoolyard, or between parent and child, teacher and child, adult friend and children.

These ways are not planned in the sense of being set. No objectives are determined nor activities planned. No one says, "Now on Tuesday morning at 10:30 A.M. I'm going to share my faith with Sue Smith."

This spontaneous sharing of faith happens when the meanings of faith are expressed in relationships and feelings. Conversations about faith and familiar words of faith may very well remain unspoken. In these times of sharing, the roles are mutual and shared, person-to-person, and not teacher-to-learner in any conscious or intentional way.

Remember the story of Jesus' disciples turning children away (Mark 10:13-16)? Jesus spoke to them and said, "Let the children come." The story goes on to say that he held, touched, and blessed the children. As I read the story, the moments described were spontaneous and unplanned.

I remember one demonstration day session with primary children. The session focused on growing and changing as a part of being created by God. It was rather carefully planned. Objectives were stated as well as ways to accomplish them. We had played a game, heard a story, made pictures of ways we had grown, and had gathered as a group on the rug to share our work. One boy rose to the occasion and organized the group for sharing—suggesting where and how the children would stand and inviting the observers to come up close and share the experience, too! That was an unplanned, spontaneous action. It was a child sharing his gifts with adults and other children. It was adults sharing their faith by allowing that child's suggestion to be implemented and their own planned closure to go by the way.

RECALL SPONTANEOUS UNPLANNED MOMENTS YOU'VE SPENT WITH CHILDREN.
What happened?

How was your faith shared? What faith meanings were communicated?

In Planned Teaching-Learning Events

I suppose when we think about ministry with children we most often think about forms of ministry that are planned. So now let's take a look at those planned times.

These ways of sharing the faith are also person-to-person. They are, however, planned and intentional. They don't just happen, although they may have moments of surprise or spontaneity within them.

In these times the adult has the role of teacher. That means planning (setting objectives and ways to accomplish them), studying, setting up the space and equipment, providing materials, introducing ideas, guiding the planning with children, listening, helping children make decisions, and evaluating.

In these events the adult is learner, too. That means listening, changing plans, being ministered to and taught by children.

In these events the adult is person. That means relating on a one-to-one basis in mutual and shared ways with other adults and children.

The teaching-learning process is experience centered. Experiences are planned that the whole group, small groups, and/or individuals can be involved in. Teachers and learners do things together. We provide opportunities for learners to do more than just hear or see, because we understand that maximum learning takes place when we experience something. The experience may be actual (for example, caring for and feeding a hamster), simulated (seeing a film of someone caring for a hamster), or imagined (imagining what it is like to take care of a hamster).

The teaching-learning process includes reflection upon the experience(s). In this part of the process we stop and look at what happened (WHAT?), we think about what it means (SO WHAT?), and consider what it will mean for our own lives when and if we do it next time (NOW WHAT?). Sometimes these steps in the process are very clear-cut and distinct. At other times they are integrated within the whole process and happen almost automatically or without being apparent to observers.

Remember the account in Luke of Jesus asking two of his followers to prepare for the Passover meal (Luke 22:7-38)? They went ahead at his direction, found the room, and made the meal preparations. Jesus and the rest of the apostles then joined Peter and John for the meal. Verse 15, ". . . I have wanted so much to eat this Passover meal with you . . . ," suggests that this was a planned event. Jesus used the meal experience to teach his followers. It was planned and intentional.

I remember a five-day lab school experience with twelve adults and fourteen four- and five-year-olds. Each day four of the twelve adults formed the teaching team, the remaining eight the observing team. On the first day our attention was drawn to a five-year-old girl (I'll call her Mary) who came into the room and spent forty minutes sitting at the book table without talking or becoming involved with anyone or anything. Her only responses were nods in reply to the lead teacher's attempts to draw her out.

For the next two days Mary sat at the same table during free play time and then did what she was asked to do when the entire group was involved together. She seemed unable to risk the possibility of relationships on her own.

The teachers next took two actions. They talked with Mary's mother and with her church school teachers, gathering information to help them plan to meet her needs.

On the fourth day it was agreed that one of the teachers would ask Mary to help her make play dough. She was asked to help, but soon other children saw what was happening and were eager to help, and Mary retreated. She sat for a while and then began to work the play dough in her hands.

In their next planning session the teachers decided that one of them would work individually with Mary. This person's objective was to draw Mary into relationship first with herself and then if possible into relationship with another child.

The following morning the teacher was waiting to greet Mary. She asked her to help prepare the morning snack. Mary nodded her agreement. She continued to nod and shrug her responses until the teacher began to phrase her questions to require a different sort of answer. Mary began to talk. She helped count the people present and even initiated relationships with other adults when supplies were needed for the snack.

Toward the end of the morning the teacher and Mary were seated in the home-living center. The teacher sat quietly. Mary was on her own, dressing and undressing a doll, and from time to time talking with another girl.

Then she turned to the teacher (who was black) and handed her a white doll, picked up a black doll for herself and said, "I have a new friend. It's you!"

The teachers made plans to let Mary receive at her own pace the faith meanings they shared. Mary used the dolls to help her tell what she could not just voice. She'd been loved and was returning love. Reflection for Mary had been taking place as she experienced caring people within the classroom.

RECALL SOME PARTICULAR TEACHING-LEARNING EVENTS YOU'VE PLANNED AND CARRIED OUT WITH CHILDREN. What happened? What faith meanings were shared in those experiences?

---

5. Where We Are Going

The objective of the church's educational ministry is
that all persons be aware of God through his self-disclosure,
    especially his redeeming love as revealed in
    Jesus Christ

                                and,

    enabled by the Holy Spirit, *respond in faith
    and love;*

                                that
as new persons in Christ they may
    know who they are and what their human
        situation means,
    grow as [children] of God rooted in the
        Christian community,
    live in obedience to the will of God in
        every relationship,
    fulfill their common vocation in the world,
                                and
    abide in the Christian hope.[1]

We are on a lifelong journey. We are helping children get started on a lifelong journey. The goal stated above describes a direction for us, gives us a standard to measure progress by, and serves as a means of evaluating our ministry with children. The goal suggests that education in the Christian community is a lifelong task. We have the possibility continually before us of growing in awareness of God and in response in faith and love.

Another way to look at the goal is to see it as valid for each stage of a person's development. Children may achieve the goal at each stage

[1] *Foundations for Curriculum* (Valley Forge: Board of Educational Ministries, American Baptist Churches, U.S.A., 1966), p. 13. (Italics added.)

of their development, granted there are different degrees of awareness and response at different stages. The differences are in terms of maturity and appropriateness of expression. The young child may easily say, "I love Jesus." The adult may say, "I'm a follower of Jesus Christ. I know that that's not an easy way." From this second perspective we can say that each of us can accomplish the goal in part, but because we change and grow we are confronted with accomplishing it anew at each new stage of our development.

Because this long-range goal is stated rather broadly and doesn't have a target date for accomplishment (except perhaps at the end of our lives), we need some short-term, clearly stated, and achievable objectives to help us measure our progress and to plan for our ministry with children. Chart B offers some clues about four areas for objectives in ministry with children. What I'd like to do at this point is to spell out what I mean by objectives, criteria for stating them, and whose responsibility they are, and to say a word about their importance in ministry with children.

A DEFINITION

Very simply *an objective is a clear statement of what we hope to accomplish.* An example from everyday life is: the evening meal (including dessert) will be on the table ready to serve and eat at 6:00 P.M. tonight. More than likely such an objective wouldn't be written down in everyday life. However, let's use it for illustrative purposes.

CRITERIA FOR OBJECTIVES

We need to see that the persons involved really *own* and agree to the objectives as stated. By owning we mean that persons understand and agree to commit themselves to the objectives. Without stating them intentionally we run the danger of each of us operating with different objectives. Using our example, consider what happens when John comes home planning to eat at 5:30 P.M. so he can be at band practice at 6:15. His parents assumed band practice was at 7:00.

HOW COULD THE FAMILY HAVE ARRIVED AT OWNERSHIP OF THE OBJECTIVE?

The objective needs to be *achievable.* It needs to be able to be accomplished within the time you have and with the skills and resources you have. Back to our illustration—Jane's job is to make an apple pie for dessert. She's late getting home from school. By the time she puts it in the oven it's 5:30 and it takes forty-five minutes to bake.

IS THE OBJECTIVE ACHIEVABLE?

What changes would make it achievable?

Objectives need to be *based on data* (information) about the participants, the planners/leaders, and the situation. The meal planner in our case study used assumed data: (1) Jane would be home from school by 3:30; (2) John's band practice was at 7:00 P.M. The meal planner did not check out the data.

HOW COULD THE MEAL PLANNER GET ACCURATE INFORMATION?

In summary we can say:
1. Objectives need to be *understood and agreed to by all persons involved.* Applying this principle to ministry with children, both children and adult leaders (the congregation too for that matter) must understand and agree to objectives. Let's be honest. Getting understanding and agreement is not easy. Ownership is something toward which we work. How we go about getting ownership and the degree to which we get it depend on many factors including the maturity of the children and adults involved.
2. Objectives need to be *achievable.* Given the resources of leaders and children, equipment and supplies available, and the time allotted, the objectives can be met.
3. Objectives are *based on data* (information) from children, the situation (group, church, or community), and the leaders. Data can first be assumed but need to be checked. There are data about: needs of children, resources (skills of both leaders and children as well as material supplies and equipment), expectations of children and leaders, wishes (what children and leaders would like to have happen), and memories of adult leaders as they recall their own experiences in the church. When you have the data, you can set objectives.

RESPONSIBILITY

Any group that plans for ministry with children needs to determine its own objectives based on data from the children in their midst. They must take into account their own strengths as planners and leaders; they must be realistic about their situation.

For example, as a national department we state objectives for our ministry with children. These objectives serve to keep us on track and to help us measure what we do. We can offer help to others in stating objectives for ministry with children but we cannot state objectives for others in their ministry with children.

Each group or person ministering with children must determine objectives appropriate for that situation, for those children, and for those leaders.

Stated objectives are useful in evaluating an event or program. We can check to see to what extent we accomplished what we started out to do. We customarily think of evaluation following an event. Checking against objectives as we go is helpful in keeping on course.

We cannot get where we are going without identifying where we want to go (or what we want to accomplish).

WHAT ARE SOME OF YOUR OBJECTIVES FOR HELPING CHILDREN RESPOND IN FAITH AND LOVE TO GOD'S REDEEMING LOVE?
(If you have no established objectives use these guidelines as you develop some.)

TO WHAT EXTENT DO THE FOLLOWING PERSONS HAVE OWNERSHIP IN THOSE OBJECTIVES?
- congregation
- leaders with children
- children

TO WHAT EXTENT ARE THE OBJECTIVES ACHIEVABLE?

UPON WHAT DATA ARE THE OBJECTIVES BASED?
- children's wishes, expectations, and needs
- adult leaders' memories, wishes, resources, and expectations
- attitudes, expectations, resources, space, equipment, and supplies of congregation

---

6. Ways to Get Where We're Going

When Alice in Wonderland met the Cheshire-Cat, she asked:

> "Would you tell me, please, which way I ought to go
> from here?"
> "That depends a good deal on where you want to get to,"
> said the Cat.
> "I don't much care where—" said Alice.
> "Then it doesn't matter which way you go," said the
> Cat.[1]

For those of us in ministry with children it does matter which way we go because we care where we're going. We've affirmed a goal about the church's educational ministry. We've said we want to help persons know and respond to God's love (see chapter 5). That's a large goal—the end goal of everything we do. We need to determine shorter range objectives to give us directions along the way and then design steps to accomplish them.

As the title of the chapter implies, there is more than one way to do ministry with children. The options are limited only by what our creativity can dream of and what the reality of our situation allows. There's usually more than one way to accomplish our objective.

To illustrate what I mean let's consider that our objective is:

> By the end of the church school year third graders will be able to identify the books of the Bible by name, briefly describe something of the contents of the books of the New Testament, and locate a reference when given book, chapter, and verse.

PROCESS

Let's take a look at a process for deciding on ways to accomplish objectives in ministry with children. Steps that I find useful are:

1. Brainstorm all the possible ways that come to mind. I like to think

[1] Lewis Carroll, *The Complete Works of Lewis Carroll* (New York: Modern Library, n.d.), pp. 71-72.

of this as the "chance to dream" stage. Every idea suggested is listed no matter how farfetched.

2. Select from the brainstorm list the ways that seem most appropriate (see pp. 41-42 for criteria for selection). I like to think of this as the "reality-testing" stage.
3. Put the items into the sequence or order that makes sense to you.
4. Plan for such details as: What resources are needed, when and for how long each thing will happen, who's responsible for it, and where it will take place.

Our brainstorm list of ways to accomplish the sample objective may look like this:

* Saturday mornings for four weeks
  a weekend retreat
* RSV copies of the Bible
* Maves' book *Finding Your Way Through the Bible*[2]
* games to make it enjoyable and fun
  film or filmstrip giving some background of the Bible
* practice sessions
* locating familiar passages
* using the table of contents
* quizzing one another
  making up own tests
* one hour each session
* imaginary or open-ended stories about authors/books of
      the New Testament

The starred items indicate those selected as ways to accomplish the objective. Our plan might develop as follows:

Learning About the Bible

A course for third graders; four Saturdays of March; 10:30-11:30 A.M. at First Baptist Church

Saturday I

Finding out what we already know—a quiz, correcting it ourselves

Getting acquainted with each other and our Bibles—everybody together (RSV Bibles needed)

Practicing identifying the books of the Bible—on our own or with a partner (copies of *Finding Your Way Through the Bible* and RSV Bibles needed)

Playing a game, "Books of the Bible"

---

[2] Paul B. Maves and Mary C. Maves, *Finding Your Way Through the Bible* (Nashville, Tenn: Abingdon Press, 1971).

Saturday II

Playing a game, "Books of the Bible"—a review

Getting acquainted with our Bibles—all together (RSV Bibles needed)

Practicing finding familiar passages giving book, chapter, and verse—on our own or with a partner (copies of *Finding Your Way Through the Bible* and RSV Bibles needed)

Playing a game, "Books, Chapters, Verses"

Saturday III

Playing a game, "Books, Chapters, Verses"—a review

Getting acquainted with the contents of the New Testament—everybody together (RSV Bibles needed, use imaginary or unfinished stories)

Practicing identifying books by contents—on your own or with a partner (RSV Bibles and work sheets needed)

Playing a Game, "What's in a Book?"

Saturday IV

Playing games—a review

Quizzing one another—each choose a reference for another to find

Finding out what we learned—using quiz given first Saturday and correcting it

Celebrating our time of learning together

What's been described above is offered as an example and is illustrative of only one way that particular objective might be accomplished. Someone else might develop the weekend retreat idea and use some of the same elements. The objective might be accomplished by using regular class time on Sunday mornings, or in a neighborhood after-school group.

CRITERIA

Once we have stated our objective, what then helps us select ways to carry out our ministries? As we choose ways to carry out our ministries with children we need to keep the following criteria in mind (use these to check the plan for "Learning About the Bible" and your own plans):

1. Is the plan appropriate for the children for whom it's designed? That is, does it fit their experiences as well as their abilities? Can they do it—not with either too much ease or too much difficulty but with just the right amount of challenge?

2. Will the plan in fact help accomplish the objective(s) set?
3. Is the plan consistent with the biblical message as understood by the planners?
4. Does the plan support the overall goal of the church's educational ministry (see chapter 5)?
5. Is implementation of the plan within the resources and skills of the persons giving leadership?
6. Is the plan possible with the money that's available?
7. Is the plan possible with the material resources available (curriculum materials, space, equipment, and supplies)?
8. Can the plan be completed within the time limits?

EXAMPLES OF WHAT'S BEING DONE OR CAN BE DONE IN MINISTRY WITH CHILDREN

The following are offered to illustrate some of the many possible ministries with children. Most have been tried or are being tried. The list is by no means conclusive. It's intended only to offer some "for instances."

Weekdays

Weekdays provide many opportunities for ministering with children. This is especially true for young children. Many churches provide weekday nursery and/or kindergarten programs for children ages three through five. These often serve both the church and the larger community. Other churches provide day-care services for working parents on a staggered fee basis, depending upon the ability to pay. One church with a weekday nursery makes its playground available to the community.[3]

After-school programs for elementary age children vary from tutoring to enrichment. Some are found in storefronts, some in church basements. Some churches offer, in addition to tutoring, a library or a reading/study room for areas not served or at a distance from a public or school library. Other churches provide space for active after-school sports and games. Still others have released-time Christian education, choir programs, or Bible study groups.

One church moved its Sunday church school for grades one to six to Tuesday afternoon. This time slot allows more time and the possibility for the pastors of the church to be involved in teaching.

[3] Playgrounds for Free is a program made possible through Playground Clearing House, Inc., under contract to Pennsylvania Department of Community Affairs. The Baptist church in Royersford, Pennsylvania, used these services in developing its playground.

Summertime

Summertime (or other vacation-from-school-times) provides the possibility for in-depth kinds of ministries. During the summer it's possible for children to be involved in day-long, overnight, or day-after-day programming. The potential for the development of a learning community is far greater than at other times. The competition for a child's time is perhaps greater, because many groups (including family, school, and community) offer other choices. We need to be sensitive to the demands upon children.

Summertime is a time for outdoor living and learning, for community building, for developing skills. It's a time for vacation church school, camping (both day and residential), and playground programs. It's a time to utilize public parks and playgrounds, front porches and backyards, city sidewalks and country fields. It's a time for ministry with neighborhood children as well.

Weekends

Sunday has been the traditional time for most of our ministry with children. Some places have as little as forty-five minutes, other places as much as two hours for church school.

It's time we looked at all the possible uses of time and space on weekends. Let's face it, forty-five minutes once a week (or for some children as little as once a month) offers limited opportunity for influencing a child. The greater impact upon a child's values and faith will come from other sources, such as family and school.

Some churches see corporate worship as well as church school as time for ministry with children. For older children there can be meaningful participation with adults in worship. Corporate worship of the congregation is then affirmed as a part of our ministry with children. In most churches we need to look at what we do when children join us for corporate worship.

Some churches utilize Sunday afternoons for church school, others for special events such as picnics and field trips. Others use Sunday evenings for supplemental education time with children. Some churches utilize Saturdays for special programs. One church in South Dakota uses a few Saturdays each year for third graders who have just received Bibles to develop skills in using them.[4] Saturdays and/or Sundays offer occasional day retreat times for older children.

In many situations Sunday time is limited because of the life-styles

[4] Linda J. Hahn, "A Bible for Every Child," *Baptist Leader* (September, 1972), pp. 57-58. The article tells about a program in First Baptist Church, Sioux Falls, South Dakota.

of the families. In such cases we need to look at how we use the time we do have as much as attempt to find other times to use.

Many churches are trying new approaches, alternate ways of conducting the Sunday church school. These include learning centers, intergenerational groupings, and family clusters.

The possibilities for ministry with children are numerous and extend beyond the Sunday church school. They are limited only by our imaginations and our resources.

IT'S YOUR TURN

I've had my say. Now it's your turn—it's time to do your own dreaming and planning. Use these chapters along with your resources as tools to help you plan with others for your ministry with children.

1. HAVE IN MIND LONG-RANGE GOALS AND STATEMENTS OF THE MISSION OF YOUR CHURCH.

2. GATHER IMPRESSIONS AND DATA ABOUT NEEDS AND RESOURCES OF CHILDREN WITH WHOM YOU WILL MINISTER.

3. GATHER DATA ON SKILLS AND STRENGTHS OF PLANNERS/LEADERS.

4. GATHER DATA ON YOUR SITUATION: ATTITUDES OF PEOPLE; THE SPACE AND EQUIPMENT AVAILABLE.

5. FROM YOUR DATA DETERMINE ACHIEVABLE OBJEC-TIVES THAT WILL ENHANCE THE FAITH DEVELOP-MENT OF THE CHILD.

6. LIST ALL POSSIBLE WAYS (sometimes called plans or strategies) TO ACCOMPLISH THOSE OBJECTIVES.

7. SELECT THE MOST APPROPRIATE ONES, ORDER THEM, AND ARRANGE FOR THE DETAILS (sometimes referred to as procedures or tactics).

8. DO IT!

9. EVALUATE, IN TERMS OF WHAT CHILDREN EXPRESS, YOUR FEELINGS AND OBSERVATIONS AND THE DEGREE TO WHICH YOU ACCOMPLISHED YOUR STATED OBJECTIVES. USE THE DATA YOU GATHER FROM THE EVALUATION TO HELP YOU DETERMINE NEXT STEPS OR WAYS TO DO ANOTHER PROGRAM.

Resource A— Bibliography

TODAY'S CHILDREN

Joseph, Stephen M., ed., *The Me Nobody Knows*. New York: Avon Books, 1972. Poems and thoughts of children from city ghettos.

Lewis, Richard, ed., *Miracles: Poems by Children of the English-Speaking World*. New York: Simon & Schuster, Inc., 1966.

GROWING, DEVELOPING PERSONS

Goldman, Ronald, *Readiness for Religion*. New York: The Seabury Press, Inc., 1970. The author has a special concern for the religious development of children.

Jenkins, William A. et al., *These Are Your Children,* 3rd ed. Glenview, Ill.: Scott, Foresman and Company, 1966. Describes what children are like at different ages and stages.

Lee, R. S., *Your Growing Child and Religion*. New York: The Macmillan Company, 1963. Describes the growth of a moral sense and an understanding of God.

ADULTS WHO MINISTER WITH CHILDREN

Jersild, Arthur T., *When Teachers Face Themselves*. New York: Teachers College Press, 1955. Discusses concerns that teachers face when they examine the meaning of who they are and what they teach.

O'Connor, Elizabeth, *Eighth Day of Creation: Gifts and Creativity*. Waco, Texas: Word, Inc., 1971. On gifts and creativity.

Rochelle, Jay C., *I'm Not the Same Person I Was Yesterday.*

Philadelphia: Fortress Press, 1974. A do-look-think-grow book offering a way to freedom.

A FAITH TO BE SHARED

Ashbrook, James B., *be/come Community*. Valley Forge: Judson Press, 1971. A book about the church to be experienced not just read.

Becker, Edwin L., *Responding to God's Call*. Valley Forge: Judson Press, 1970. The nature of God's work in the world and human responses for our day.

Clark, M. Edward, *Experience-Centered Learning for Church Leaders*. Valley Forge: Board of Educational Ministries, American Baptist Churches, 1970. Describes a way of learning by doing.

Hazelton, Roger, *Knowing the Living God*. Valley Forge: Judson Press, 1969. Investigates what it means that God is alive and how he can be known.

Rood, Wayne R., *On Nurturing Christians*. Nashville, Tenn.: Abingdon Press, 1972. Author encourages us to reclaim our ability to nurture.

Thurman, Howard, *The Centering Moment*. New York: Harper & Row, Publishers, 1969. Meditations and prayers for personal reflection.

WHERE WE'RE GOING

Blazier, Kenneth, and Huber, Evelyn, *Planning Christian Education in Your Church*. Valley Forge: Judson Press, 1974. Guide for planning the year.

"The Church's Ministry with Children: An Administrative Packet." Valley Forge: Board of Educational Ministries, American Baptist Churches, U.S.A., 1973. Ideas about children, programs, space, and equipment, etc.

WAYS TO GET WHERE WE'RE GOING

"Church Options for Day Care." Philadelphia: Geneva Press,

1973. Pamphlets and booklets with guidance for those considering day-care programs.

Florence, Nan, *Vacation—A Time for Learning.* Nashville, Tenn.: Abingdon Press, 1969. A manual for vacation church schools and other summertime settings.

Hathaway, Lulu, *Partners in Teaching Older Children.* Valley Forge: Judson Press, 1971. A manual for those who work with middlers and juniors.

Hemphill, Martha Locke, *Partners in Teaching Young Children.* Valley Forge: Judson Press, 1972. For workers with kindergarten and primary children.

__________, *Weekday Ministry with Young Children.* Valley Forge: Judson Press, 1973. A manual for the church weekday nursery school.

Johnson, Ronald K., *Planning Outdoor Christian Education.* Philadelphia: United Church Press, 1972. An administrative guide for planners of outdoor experiences with older elementary girls and boys.

Martin, C. Lewis, and Travis, John T., *Exceptional Children: A Special Ministry.* Valley Forge: Judson Press, 1968. Describes ministries with handicapped persons in which local churches can engage.

Purchase, Richard and Betty, *Let's Go Outdoors with Children.* Philadelphia: The Westminster Press, 1972. An administrative guide for grades one to four.

Using Learning Centers in Church Education. A thirty-page booklet from Joint Educational Development, Designs for Children's Ministry series, John Knox Press, 1973.

Wangner, Florence E., *Resource Portfolio of Nursery Education Handbooks.* Valley Forge: Board of Educational Ministries, American Baptist Churches, U.S.A., 1968. Ten handbooks on such subjects as storytelling, room arrangements, and children ages two to four.

Resource B—
A Checklist

One way to get information about needs in relation to ministry with children in your church is to use a checklist such as the following. Parents, teachers, and/or the whole congregation could be asked to complete such a checklist.

1. Our church enables the faith development of children in these areas (check the appropriate column):

	We do this well	We're not doing well
relationship to God through Jesus	__________	__________
relationship to the church	__________	__________
relationship to the Bible	__________	__________
relationship to others	__________	__________

2. The strongest part of our ministry with children is. . . .

3. The weakest part of our ministry with children is. . . .

4. Ministry with children has (high) (low) priority in our church budget. Circle one.

5. The persons who work with children in our church (check one)
   _______ are enthusiastic about their work
   _______ are discouraged
   _______ can't wait to be replaced when their "term" is up

6. The congregation is aware and supportive of what we are trying to do in children's ministry (check one).
   _______ Most members are aware and supportive.
   _______ Probably half of the members know what we're trying to do.
   _______ Only a few members know or care about ministry with children.

7. What one thing would you like to see changed within the next year?